BLINDED

MATURED FOR PURPOSE

DR. JAVASKI D. MCDONALD

Editor: Nathan Bustillos
Formatting: Brady Moller

CONTENTS

More grace to everyone who wants to take charge
of their life,
I further want to dedicate
this book to my Mother and Grandmothers,
and
my family, my Pastors, my Mentors,
and to all
Across the world

FOREWORD
REVEREND MARK D. PECINA

As a senior pastor of 25 years and over 45 years of ministry experience, I have come to acknowledge one of the biggest struggles believers face is spiritual blindness. Spiritual blindness occurs when we are unable to see God or understand His message. People often fail to acknowledge God is constantly working on our behalf. He pursues us daily and desires to show us His glory. When we are spiritually blinded, it often carries great consequence. The bible declares that one who does not see God, is doing it willingly because they choose not to give it serious attention.

"If our Message is obscure to anyone, it's not because we're holding back in any way. No, it's because these other people are looking or going the wrong way and refuse to give it serious attention. All they have eyes for is the fashionable god of darkness. They think he can give them what they want, and that they won't have to bother believing a Truth they can't see. They're stone-blind to the dayspring brightness of the Message that shines with Christ, who gives us the best picture of God we'll ever get."

— 2 CORINTHIANS 4: 3-4 MSG

Five years ago, when I met Dr. JaVaski McDonald, he was an up-and-coming minister and student. He had all the zeal, but lacked the spiritual awakening. Serving as his Spiritual Father, I walked alongside him closely. I saw first-hand the tears, fears, and epiphanies shared within the pages of this book. I also witnessed him grow spiritually by leaps and bounds. This is a reflective journal of daily living and moments of spiritual revelations given to him by God through trial and error.

It is very common for people to have tunnel vision and the desire to only see it one way. Their way. You may have all the good intentions in the world and say, "I will never be spiritually blind." You are already being deceived because spiritual blindness can come packaged in many different ways. 2 Corinthians 4:4, tells us that the god of this world will do everything in his power to keep us from seeing the truth. The belief that you can do it your way and think you'll be satisfied, will set you up to fail. The devil wants you to live a life with distorted vision. He will make efforts to immobilize you by loading you down with all sorts of bondage and you won't have the vision to see the truth about who you are in God.

This book will help you learn to listen and perceive the message God is speaking. ***Blinded: Matured for Purpose*** will assist you and give you the necessary tools to walk in agreement with God. Your journey in this life can shed light to your possibilities or consume you with guilt and shame.

Choose you this day to stop being BLINDED.

-Reverend Mark D. Pecina
Founder and Senior Pastor
Faith Builders Worship Center, Buda, TX

PRAISE FOR BLINDED

"*The educational value of the book for the young and old is obvious. Dr. McDonald is transparent and reveals the journey of his growth. Blinded, Matured for Purpose reminds readers of the greatness of God and the benefits of traveling with eyes wide open. Thank you Dr. JaVaski for your candidness and willingness to be vulnerable for the betterment of the kingdom of God. I recommend this book for personal reflection and for group discussions.*"

REV. DR. NATHAN J. ROBERTSON, JR
EXECUTIVE PASTOR, ST. JAMES BAPTIST
CHURCH, AUSTIN, TX CHAPLAIN, AUSTIN
FIRE DEPARTMENT

XI

"Dr. JD McDonald presents a perfect picture of the internal battle we all face in following God's will and practical insights on how to overcome the battle within. A must-read for anyone looking to pursue God's purpose for their life."

PASTOR BRIAN SISNEROS
FOUNDER AND LEAD PASTOR ACCESS
CHURCH DEL RIO, TX & EAGLE PASS, TX

"It's always a joy to hear about the transforming power of the love of Jesus. Thank you for making it plain by shedding light on practical ways of yielding to the Holy Spirit in our everyday lives. From darkness to light, once blind but now to be able to see so clearly that God had a plan all along. Proud of you my brother!"

PASTOR "KENNY WAYNE" SMITH
FOUNDER & LEAD PASTOR HOPE NATION
CHURCH, AUSTIN, TX

"This book is an encouraging eye-opener. Dr. JaVaski, you are truly a blessing. This book is going to help people struggling with disappointment, brokenness, and disobedience. It reminds us that in difficult times, God

is still there. God will use your pain to be a testimony to others. Dr. McDonald, I am so proud of what God is doing in your life. You're truly helping others and His purpose and plan shall be fulfilled. Congratulations."

"MAMA APOSTLE LUCY BONA"
FOUNDER OF INTERNATIONAL BROKEN
HEART HEALING AND RESTORATION
MINISTRIES, AUSTIN, TX

"Blinded, Matured for Purpose, reminds us of God's beloved promise to remain by our side at all times. Throughout our spiritual journey, the growing pains can seem unbearable. Push and pray! You are being refined and developed with purpose! I pray that this book blesses every reader and you remain encouraged after your vision is restored. Dr. JD, thank you for the reminder that tough times "won't last always", but God's love and faithfulness is everlasting."

MELISSA J. MARTINI M.A.
EDITOR, TEACHER.
SAN, ANTONIO, TX

Dr. JaVaski's Blinded is an amazing inspirational book for all! It will encourage you, uplift you, and inspire you to let go of all the ideologies that keep us from hearing God's voice and following God's purpose for our lives. This book is an easy read yet extremely thought-provoking and life-changing. A must-have!

COACH TIAUDRA TAYLOR
B.S. PSYCHOLOGY
INTERNATIONAL CERTIFIED LIFE COACH
ELLICOTT CITY, MARYLAND

YOU GOT THIS!

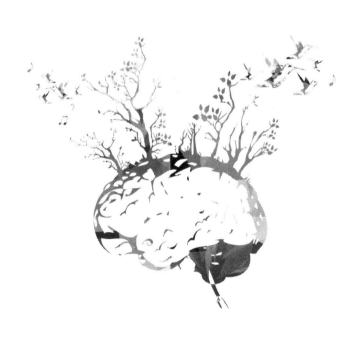

PREFACE

Encouragement

This book's purpose is to inspire you along
your journey.
It's meant to be passed along to someone
that needs to be uplifted and encouraged
through their process in life.
I want you to know that God is Serious
about you!

INTRODUCTION

In reading this book, I pray for God's Guidance to help you wipe the slate clean. I pray for God's will to be done as you navigate through the constant battle between your heart, emotions, God's divine will, love, and protection.

I can remember like it was yesterday. I was kneeling in prayer beside my bed, and at that moment, my heart was just broken. As I prayed, God presented me with a vision of a pathway, which led to Jesus' tomb. I noticed people walking in one by one and they were being welcomed. The light illuminating from the tomb beamed so beautifully, and I wanted to be in the glory of God too. When I attempted to walk and join them, I was immobile. I was stagnant. I literally could not move. It was as if something was grabbing hold of me, preventing me from moving forward. Internally, it felt like I was holding onto unnecessary things, and those things were keeping me anchored in my current state.

As I remained upon my knees, praying, and crying, this is when God spoke to me. He told me I could no longer be blinded by my own desires and emotions. A change had to occur, and I had to really examine myself. My way of living and my way of thinking needed to be adjusted. You have to live in truth so you can see clearly!

"In their case the god of this world has blinded the minds of the unbelievers, to keep them from seeing the light of the gospel of the glory of Christ, who is the image of God."

— 2 CORINTHIANS 4:4 ESV

In that moment, I realized my distorted vision and selfish ways stood in the way of receiving the glory and gifts God wanted for me. The Lord wanted me to release all the bondage that was keeping me from fulfilling my purpose, and to see things through the lens of Christ. In the bible, we learned about Saul's conversion, and like many of us, Saul was blinded. When he was able to see clearly, he learned God was the true purpose in his life. Sometimes, you'll have an encounter with God that will change the way you look at life and the way you look at Him. Sometimes, those encounters are so powerful, you'll be filled with a conviction and it will completely change your whole outlook on life.

"As he neared Damascus on his journey, suddenly a light from heaven flashed around him. He fell to the ground and heard a voice say to him, "Saul, Saul, why do you persecute me?"

— ACTS 9:3-4

Get ready, because now it's time to see!

This is a book of significant value. It is intended to help open your eyes, mind, and heart to Jesus. I pray you are placed within the protection of God, and free from the devices of the devil. Blindness is the form of disbelief, so I pray you grow and mature in life with the elevation of God and all He desires for you. I, too, have been through countless deceptions, self-infliction, self-sabotage, persecution, condemnation, lies, lustful infatuations, and deceit. But I can testify and assure you, God has saved my life.

If I would have submitted to God and listened to His words and direction earlier in life, it would have been a lot less painful and a speedier trip to receiving the abundance He had in store.

> *"Do not conform of this world but be transformed by the renewing of your mind. Then you will be able to test and approve what God's will is—His good, pleasing and perfect will."*
>
> — *ROMANS 12:2*

He saved me and will save you too! I hope to give you impartation, and pour into your lives through my experiences as a servant of the Lord. I pray you're guided righteously on your journey in life and the choices you make, the crossroads you choose, and the desires of your heart always lead you to Christ Jesus.

You have a decision to make!

I

BLINDED

"He has blinded their eyes and hard-ened their heart, lest they see with their eyes, and understand with their heart, and turn, and I would heal them."

—JOHN 12:40

When I was younger, God would speak to my heart and think through my mind, but because of the state I was in, I didn't always understand or see things clearly. If I knew then what I know now, I would have made better choices. Blindness is really nothing more than an avoidance of our sins. People who are blinded focus more on the negative, rather than the greater things in their life. This type of mindset can lead you into a deep, dark pit. I didn't just have poor vision through the use of my physical eyes, but I also hadn't developed spiritual maturity yet. As I reflect on my younger years, I realize I had unfiltered desires as I chased and idolized success in secular music. I had a profound love for listening to and creating music, and while I was traveling across the country on tour, I turned a blind eye to what God desired for me. I was living two lives. I was a music artist and a man who desired a greater connection with the Lord. But the reality of my situation was that the two worlds couldn't coexist. I was torn between a life that followed Jesus and a life that followed my emotions and desires. The conflict started affecting me, and I started to lose things in my life. There was a season where I was transitioning. In that transition, I was homeless, sleeping in my car. I was a few months behind on my car note with an unimpressive credit score, asking to sleep on the floor of my friends' and family members' homes. It felt like everything I touched, I broke. Everything that was connected to me seemed to be ruined or it wasn't flourishing. The enemy and my desires pulled me away from the security and the presence of God and I wasn't prospering as I should.

My Grandmother remained in prayer, and interceded on my behalf. She would call me with words of encouragement and pray over me daily, reminding me that troubled times "won't last always." When you're blinded, you don't have the vision to recognize it, because you're operating with immature vision.

> *"The enemy is a deceiver, a manipulator who operates to kill, steal, and destroy."*
>
> *— JOHN 10:10*

I was spiritually immature, and God knew what I needed to see and learn for myself. I had to go through it in order to grow through it. Thankfully, God intervened to redirect my path by removing the blinders that restricted me from seeing the abundance He intended for me. He brought me to a humble place, spoke to my heart, and provided a place of clarity and understanding. The knowledge of God will keep you from being spiritually blinded. Many assume fearing the Lord is a threatening tactic, but we fear the Lord because we love and respect His covering, and so we cannot reject the knowledge He gives us, but instead we should honor it. We should embrace His wisdom, His growth in you, & His council.

"The fear of the Lord is the beginning of knowledge, but fools despise wisdom."

— *PROVERBS 1:7*

In my youth, my undeveloped understanding and immaturity resulted in prayers asking for God to improve my relationships and straighten up my life emotionally and financially, in hopes it would improve my situation as a whole. God would tell me to seek Him first. As I think back, it was really self-induced blindness, which is nothing more than a way of avoiding sins and the avoidance of seeing yourself for who you really are.

"And if your eye causes you to sin, gouge it out and throw it away. It's better to enter eternal life with only one eye than to have two eyes and be thrown into the fire of hell."

— *MATTHEW 18:9*

4

> ***"Whatever the heart thinketh, so is he."***
>
> — ***PROVERBS 23:7***

Biblically, the ones who walk in the darkness of ignorance are blinded. We tend to overlook the truth, and ignoring the signs and your God-given discernment is ignoring the message God has placed in your heart. Our hearts become trained and conditioned throughout life, but God wants us to live in truth. When we reside in truth, it allows us to be free. Once you overlook a situation and make it greater than God, it becomes an idol.

What do I mean? Well... I'm glad that you asked! The bible says,

> ***"You shall have no other gods before me. You shall not make for yourself a carved image, or any likeness of anything that is in heaven above, or that is in the earth beneath, or that is in the water under the earth. You shall not bow down to them or serve them, for I the Lord your God am a jealous God."***
>
> — ***EXODUS 20:3-5***

This is a really critical part of your life. This stronghold will cause you to reject the covering and protection of God's merciful and grateful hand. Here are a few simple but deeper questions for you about idols:

1. **What have you put before God?**
2. **Where are you now and how do you feel?**
3. **Why are you choosing to go back into it?**
4. **Why is that fulfilling a thirst in your life?**

This often happens in love and deception, inviting troubles, cycles, and chaos to take hold of your life. The enemy will take advantage of your spiritual immaturity and entice you with physical things that you'll desire, lust, and overstretch for, in an effort to destroy you. I remember when my brother said, "You can't lay down with snakes and expect to be healed. You're going to get bitten and you're going to be ill". It's like being on a ship that keeps wavering back and forth, distorting your perception. I was blinded by selfish desires and my wrong thinking patterns. When you sit at the enemy's table, you forget you have Kingship and a greater calling because you continue to see your-self so much smaller than the way God sees you. You perceive things by emotions rather than truth, and God wants you to follow the truth. You must be protective by thinking and acting more like Christ.

> *"Then you will know the truth, and the truth will set you free."*
>
> — *JOHN 8:32*

In the parable of the Prodigal Son, he was spiritually blinded until he came to himself. We can be living in a world feasting amongst pigs, and we fail to realize our real worth and value because of that blindness. We might lose all of our posses-sions and reside in pure chaos, but God is so faith-ful, loving, and forgiving. The knowledge of God will heal you, if you listen. The question is, Don't you want to obtain that knowledge? Freedom from captivity. Free from the desires of the flesh, wrong environments, unfulfilling and draining employment. Free from bondage, neglect, verbal abuse, Jezebel, Delilah, narcissists, and the many demonic spirits that wanted and attempted to destroy you. When we come to ourselves, we must learn from the hard lessons, but ultimately they are worth it. Spiritual blindness creates illusions and delusions far from where God wants you to be. Once you see yourself clearly, elevation will begin. You'll obtain new, purposeful knowledge and understanding under the direction of Christ.

> *"Consider it pure joy, my brothers and sisters, whenever you face trials of many kinds, because you know that the testing of your faith produces persever-ance. Let perseverance finish its work so that you may be mature and complete, not lacking anything."*
>
> *— JAMES 1:2-4*

Know this: You cannot ignore the truth. Allow the knowledge of God to heal you.

Daily Prayer: *"Lord reveal what's in me, so that I can see Your truth."*

2

ARE YOU IN THE CYCLE

L ooking back over my experiences, others' experiences, and the countless conversations I've had over the years, I've noticed a lot of familiar traits. Failure to recognize the choices which initiate problems and confusion in our lives gives the enemy opportunity to latch and attach itself to our weaknesses. There are so many distractions that will work to steer you off the course of what God has destined for you and your future.

"But I have this complaint against you. You are permitting that woman—that Jezebel who calls herself a prophet—to lead my servants astray. She teaches them to commit sexual sin and to eat food offered to idols."

— *REVELATION 2:20*

LATCH INTO THE CYCLE

Many define insanity as the act of performing the same actions over and over again with the expectation of a different outcome. In life, we are sometimes paralyzed in this state of stagnation or we remain in a damaging environment, repeating a cycle of unhealthy behaviors that impedes our spiritual growth. Oftentimes, we are drawn to familiar spirits. They'll attach themselves to areas of interest and we invite them in. You have to be more cautious! When we don't have clarity, we will sometimes return to what makes us sick because of comfortability and confusion, but God is so faithful. He'll provide us with knowledge and understanding, but unfortunately, for many of us, because of our foolish, selfish, and disobedient ways, we don't even realize God is trying to save us.

> *"There hath no temptation taken you but such as is common to man: but God is faithful, who will not suffer you to be tempted above that ye are able; but will with the temptation also make a way to escape, that ye may be able to bear it."*
>
> — *1 CORINTHIANS 10:13*

God loves me and has saved me from many disobedient failures, so I can offer you my own personal testimony in hopes of assuring you of His unwavering love for you. I was once severely blinded and caught in a demonic cycle that intended to harm me and keep me from His glory. I stopped seeing myself as a king and royal priesthood in God's Kingdom, and instead idolized my relationships. It was as if I was laying in the snake pit being bitten repeatedly, as my brother explained. I was lost and wandering aimlessly in a disoriented state. During this time, God presented me with a vision. I didn't understand the significance behind it until I went into scripture to understand the crippling ways of my repetitive behaviors. In this vision, the Lord presented me with a man clothed all in white, kneeling beside a riverbank. As he stroked his hand through the water, I realized the waters were muddy. As I watched him sway with his hands playing in the mud, the man turned his attention towards me and rose to his feet. As he looked in my direction, he gazed upon me with a look of anger on his face that I'll never forget. I struggled to understand why God gave me this vision. Few nights I prayed and pondered over this vision, but as I studied my bible, I came across these two passages:

> *"Like a dog that returns to its vomit, So is a fool who repeats his foolishness."*
>
> — *PROVERBS 26:11*

> *"of them the proverbs are true: 'A dog returns to its vomit,' and, 'A sow that is washed returns to her wallowing in the mud."*
>
> — *2 PETER 2:22, NIV:*

Now, take a moment and read those again.

I want it to provide unction in your spirit.

Now, process it. Ok! Here we go.

In other words, you foolishly keep going back to the root of your sickness, the source of your impairment, and the very thing God is trying to save you from.

Those scriptures stuck with me that day, and every day after, because you cannot ignore chaos when God reveals it to you. I sat and I wept because God spoke to me so boldly. He loudly encouraged me to go a different route, because I had steered off His path and where I was going wasn't meant for me. I journaled about the vision God gave me, in hopes that it would help me make sense of what God was saying. In doing so, this scripture surfaced in my heart as I was writing:

"My people are destroyed for lack of knowledge: because thou hast rejected knowledge."

— HOSEA 4:6 KJV

The knowledge and crushing I received were

necessary because now I know what it looks like to be in a battle and how to come out victoriously. If you choose to remain in harm's way, it can potentially break a special part of you, and kill your confidence. But again, God is faithful! If you only knew what He has planned for you, you'd understand why He continuously offers His protection and fights for your peace. You have to reclaim your position in His Kingdom and place the crown back upon your head. You must believe it mentally, physically, and spiritually, because God has divine plans for you that won't include turmoil, pain, or suffering. We have to accept the truth and understand that we cannot change people. God does that. God loves them too, so you have to be careful what you're asking for. Their rationale and actions may not be in agreement with what God has willed for their life. You deserve to see His plan through.

One thing I know for sure, God saved me. He saved me from myself, and I know He will save you too. My hope is that you experience less pain and turmoil, and these words help you get out of any cycle that seeks to harm you. With the Lord's help and guidance, I was saved from my situation, and here's what helped deliver me:

1. PRAY. No, really, PRAY. Pray without ceasing.

A relationship and communication with God will lead you to salvation. That is what He really desires of you. Nothing should ever supersede His excellence. We require food and water to sustain and function properly, mentally and physically. Prayer should be greater than both. Prayer nourishes your mind, body, soul, and spirit.

"Pray without ceasing"

— *1 THESSALONIANS 5:17 ESV*

"And whatever you ask in prayer, you will receive if you have faith."

— *MATTHEW 21:22 ESV*

2. You have to flee to be free. I mean RUN! Really, run, and don't look back.

The truth is everyone and everything isn't operating in the mindset of Christ. If we play in the wilderness with people who do not act out of love and in the will of Christ, you can be in dangerous territory. We cannot play games with something so callous. The enemy does not care about what you have, what you look like, or how you feel. The enemy doesn't care about you at all. We have to remove ourselves from things, people, and situations that are harmful and displeasing to God.

"Submit yourselves, then, to God. Resist the devil, and he will flee from you."

— *JAMES 4:7*

There is a saying, "hurt people, hurt people." When someone treats you in a harmful manner, it's not just them, but what's in them which they conformed to. I was on the receiving end of somebody else's pain, and unfortunately, I had to experience their trauma over and over before I understood I was in the wrong territory. We will have those moments when we come to ourselves and realize the bondage that's keeping us from God's plan and purpose. We need to be in an agreement with God, obey, and listen to his directives. God is action-driven. If you're praying for change and deliverance, God can and will intervene boldly. The way you protect yourself from danger and harm is by saying YES to God and NO to destructive cycles.

"No temptation has overtaken you that is not common to man. God is faithful, and he will not let you be tempted beyond your ability, but with the temptation, he will also provide the way of escape, that you may be able to endure it."

— *1 CORINTHIANS 10:13*

When temptation is upon us, He will always provide a way of escape. Use your God-given discernment and move when God says move, because He is serious about you. So SERIOUS about you.

Know this: You can't compromise. You have too much to lose.

Daily Prayer: *"Father God, thank you for giving me the way out. I cannot allow my flesh to be weak."*

3

ARE YOU HEARING GOD, OR ARE YOU LISTENING

Question - are you just hearing, or are you *listening*? Like, really *listening*? What does that mean to you? I remember when my mother would say to me, "It seems as if everything I say to you goes from one ear and out the other - you have to start listening to me." My response was always, "Mom, I am hearing you," knowing I didn't wash the dishes or take out the trash that night. It was a lesson that was brought to my attention at a young age; listening is very important. I want to give you this simple knowledge: hearing is defined as the ability to perceive sound, and listening is the ability to accurately receive the message in communication. In this case, everything that we hear doesn't always have a purpose, but everything you listen to will always give you understanding. In the bible, it speaks about how God will speak through visions and dreams to the prophets in the old and new testament. They would be able to communicate and listen to God through these visions and dreams.

> *"And in the last days it shall be, God declares, that I will pour out my Spirit on all flesh, and your sons and your daughters shall prophesy, and your young men shall see visions, and your old men shall dream dreams."*
>
> — *ACTS 2:17 (ESV)*

If you are hearing something, that's one thing. If you're hearing by faith, then you're now listening to what God has said to you. The bible says faith cometh by hearing and hearing by the word of God. As you get older, and start dealing with relationships, jobs, kids, your household, etc., that is when you'll start to learn. For me, I wasn't truly listening to God as I should when He was protecting and advancing my life. But here are a few things that helped me become more disciplined when listening:

1. Humble Yourself.

Humbling yourself and removing any agenda allows God to speak directly to you. He will take over the conversations.

> *"And when you pray, do not heap up empty phrases as the Gentiles do, for they think that they will be heard for their many words. Do not be like them, for your Father knows what you need before you ask him."*
>
> — *MATTHEW 6:7-8 (ESV)*

We all want answers to our prayers, but God will provide it. Life is a long, beautiful journey. It's a heavenly marathon - not an empty sprint.

2. Go to Your Quiet Place.

There's intimacy in your quiet place that will allow you to ask God for clarity. Ask God what He's trying to show and tell you. Give him more than ten minutes of your time, and He will begin to speak to your heart. Some people spend hours with God to get better understanding and be in

His presence. If His presence is not there, be patient and wait on Him. He will show himself.

> *"Here's what I want you to do: Find a quiet, secluded place so you won't be tempted to role-play before God. Just be there as simply and honestly as you can manage. The focus will shift from you to God, and you will begin to sense his grace."*
>
> — *MATTHEW 6:6 MSG*

3. Ask God for Clarity.

As you're building your relationship with God, you will learn to submit yourself to the words that He told you. Sometimes, we're not sure of the message, so asking for clarity isn't wrong. There are examples of a need for clarity in the bible, like when Gideon asked God for a sign:

"Then Gideon said to God, 'Please don't be angry with me, but let me make one more request. Let me use the fleece for one more test. This time let the fleece remain dry while the ground around it is wet with dew.' 40 So that night God did as Gideon asked. The fleece was dry in the morning, but the ground was covered with dew."

— **JUDGES 6:39-40**

Take your time and make sure you have a clear understanding. Listening obediently will help strengthen and develop your relationship with God. Sometimes, God will present you with a big decision that will change the trajectory of your life. In those moments, you need to ask yourself: are you hearing, or are you *listening* to God?

Know this: Establish your prayer life.

Daily Prayer: *"Father God, allow me to be able to hear you and open the eyes to my heart. Convict me."*

4

IN MY FLESH

Oh, my flesh… Oh, my flesh… What to do with this flesh? I know many of us say and think that day in and day out. **The meaning of "Flesh" is thus credited with the emotions and responses of the whole person**. Stop and think about the why. Why does your whole being get into sticky situations, and why am I being chained to the individual or situation? Why would I want to put myself in harm's way?

This is a significant prayer I say often, "**Oh Lord protect me from me.**" I want you to repeat that again slowly… ask yourself if this is definitely worth my life? Is it worth going into, or is it worth returning into something again? You're going to have to make a critical choice. You have to choose if you're going to follow your flesh or follow what God says. Everyone isn't following after the heart of God, and following God's command will save time, energy, and your whole life. My natural father would say this quote, "You can lie to everybody else, but can't lie to yourself." In other words, you keep hiding your truth physically, but you can't hide what you're dealing with inside. Hence, the flesh. The bible says,

"My child, listen when your father corrects you. Don't neglect your mother's instruction."

— *PROVERBS 1:8*

As a teenager, I lost my mother. I remember her teaching me the importance of being a good young man, and doing the right thing regardless of whatever other people choose to do. I recall weeks before my mother passed, we sat in conversation and she told me, "Always remember to ask God to guide you." God knows which way to go when people don't. Although I made plenty of unwise decisions in my life, the evidence has shown true. I followed my emotions for an extensive percentage of my life, and it led me to heartbreak and hardships. This can happen at any stage of life. I think about the text in the bible that says, **"The fear of the Lord is the beginning of wisdom and knowledge."** The knowledge of God will protect you from spiritual blindness and your fleshly desires daily.

> *"I have been crucified with Christ, and I no longer live, but Christ lives in me. The life I live in the body, I live by faith in the Son of God, who loved me and gave Himself up for me."*
>
> — *GALATIANS 2:20*

We have to take charge of this area of our lives. It's the flesh that will have us doing unspeakable things. David cried out seeking forgiveness for his sins. He said, "**for I acknowledge my transgressions: and my sin is ever before me.**" Meaning, I knew the sin I was doing before I did it, and still didn't stop. Let me share this analogy with you: whatever you think in your mind, your body follows, so whatever you choose in your mind, your body will respond. When you respond to God's command, you are choosing the right insight and promising direction. So, how are you going to respond?

Ways to respond:

1. Make the hard decision. It will save your life. Asking yourself is this worth my life? *Matthew 16:26 "And what do you benefit if you gain the whole world but lose your own soul?"* Is anything worth more than your soul?

2. Be Encouraged: Know that God is with you and He loves and wants to see you succeed. *Deuteronomy 31:6 "Be strong and courageous. Do not fear or be in dread of them, for it is the Lord your God who goes with you. He will not leave you or forsake you."*

3. Stop being afraid. *2 Timothy 1:7 "God didn't create the spirit of fear but of power, love, and a sound mind."* Let your mind be sound, have self-control, self-discipline.

You can overcome what is not for you. Don't

let your flesh consume you. Repent and turn away from it.

Know this: **You have too much to lose!**

Daily Prayer: *"Oh Lord God, protect me from me."*

5

THE TERRITORY

You. YES, YOU! Get out of the wrong territory. Walking in the wrong territory is like being in a room or a system you don't belong in. Your eyes can see things that seem dysfunctional and out of place, and you can tell when there's disorder in the room. You can also tell when there's affliction in a person too. You may be walking into a system of blinded beliefs, and you have to be mindful about what you're entering into and know how to safely and quickly evacuate. Many territories don't have the capacity to carry good things in them because of the beliefs of the system. It's an unhealthy environment, and you have to move along. If you're in the wrong territory, it prevents you from seeing clearly, but when you're in alignment with where

God desires you to be, and you've stepped into territories where you belong, you'll feel comfort and have the discernment to recognize the difference between the two. The closer you get to God, iniquity can't be with you.

Throughout the bible, it discusses territory and possession of the territory. You cannot just enter without permission. Just like the story of Moses freeing the Israelites from the territory of the blinded Pharaoh, whose heart was hardened. Moses led the people to the promised land, and in order for that to happen, they had to leave the territory that enslaved and kept them in bondage. If you find yourself stuck in the mental and physical forms of captivity, you're operating in other people's dysfunctional territory and it's time for you to be free.

> *"For freedom Christ has set us free; stand firm therefore, and do not submit again to a yoke of slavery."*
>
> — *GALATIANS 5:1 ESV*

Whose system are you operating in? Is it a system that's bringing sickness to your life and your thought process? Is the person or people

BLINDED: MATURED FOR PURPOSE

you're around bringing you away from God, or bringing you closer to God? Whose system are you truly operating in? Are you following and trusting God enough to say, "I can't be a part of something that is going to break me or put me in bondage or captivity for my life."? The territory that you choose, and the system that you are engaging with can either make you sick or heal you. Who and what is building you up? Who and what is helping you with your healing process? When God is the main focus, then the individuals around you should be flowing along with you to help you go along on your journey. In this journey called life,

"I will trust in the Lord with all my heart and lean not to my own understanding and acknowledge Him, He will direct your path."

— PROVERB 3:5-6

When you operate in God's obedience, you operate with full confidence by faith that God will get you there, regardless of what you see around you. Remain faithful in prayer, and ask God to keep you protected. Ask Him to keep you, so that you remain in the territory that God has already purposed for you.

Daily Prayer:

"Please bless me by enlarging my territory. May your hand be with me! Keep me from harm, so that it will not cause me pain."

— *1 CHRONICLES 4:10*

Know this: God will save your life from bondage.

Daily Prayer: *"Father God, give me the understanding, knowledge, and strength to not walk into the wrong territory."*

6

STANDING IN AGREEMENT

Be in unison with God! No matter what comes along in your life. When you're in agreement with God, this is your place of safety and protection. Being in agreement with God is the meaning to have a full understanding of what God says and how he said it to you. God is against confliction, but wants you to receive conviction.

> **"I will say of the LORD, 'He is my refuge and my fortress, my God, in whom I trust.'"**
>
> — **PSALMS 9:2**

Trusting the voice of the Father is more

important than trusting the voice of a person. Nothing should supersede God's voice and what He shares with you. It's the unction that God gives you to keep you on track and align you with Him. Standing in agreement is eliminating the loud distractions. Standing in agreement with God is the way that you continue to uphold yourself, by binding and loosening things that should not have authority to control your life. When you're binding and loosening things over your life, you're able to fight against the devices of the enemy. Those are things that bring clutter and confusion to your heart, and into your mind. Those circumstances will overwhelm your life, and should not have a home there. Sometimes, you'll recall something that was said to you when you were younger that affected you. It's important to stand in agreement with God because otherwise, you're believing in an old system. God is putting you in a new system, which will allow you to go places, and He'll elevate you to higher levels of advancement. Standing in agreement with God is faithfulness, and the belief that He'll add to your life. He's going to deepen your levels of knowledge and understanding.

Know this: What God has for you will align you with your purpose.

Daily Prayer: *"Lord, bless me not to be in contention with you and I do what you say over my flesh and what the world does."*

7

THIS HAS ONLY MADE YOU STRONGER

I know it hurts, but it only makes you stronger. You can now recognize the capability and the strength you have to endure to the end. That hurt has equipped you to become better no matter if the person hurt you, left you, or if people deceived you. Maybe the job let you go and you had to learn how to pick up the pieces on your own. It only made you stronger.

"Consider it pure joy, my brothers and sisters, whenever you face trials of many kinds, because you know that the testing of your faith produces perseverance. Let perseverance finish its work so that you may be mature and complete, not lacking anything."

— JAMES 1:2-4 NIV

Perseverance through faith is what developed your strength and allowed you to see how far you can go; how far you can reach and that God's hand of Grace is over your life. I remember a conversation I had with a friend who was battling cancer. They were dealing with so much fear, but believed God would heal them so they could leave the hospital completely healed and set free. We believed God would remove any sickness, and so we prayed daily, trusting it was already done. God did His perfect will and He healed my friend, leaving behind the imprint of His power and confidence to trust in Him at all times. Their faith in God allowed them to understand the strength that they carry in their life. Hear this! It only made you stronger. It only made you stronger because you're now realizing how hard the enemy was trying to stop you from reaching your destination.

During the time I was homeless, it was such a low point in my life, but I remember when my Grandmother said to me, "You got this! And you have to get up, baby!" Her words and prayers were the encouragement I needed. Although I didn't recognize it at the time, my strength was being developed in those moments. Diamonds are created under pressure and the levels that God has for you exceed what you've ever seen before. It exceeds the place your family thought you would be. It exceeds the place your friends thought you were going to go, or even the critics that sat on the sidelines watching and waiting to see you fail, but God has a plan for you. You had to go through it. You had to face adversity. You had to chase after the dream that God has for you. That's why the enemy wanted to distract you, so you wouldn't be able to see the full vision of what God's already given for you and your life. So, I wanted to let you know again, this only made you stronger. Those weeks or months that felt like you were going through depression and heartache, and maybe even rage, God was still whispering in your ear. Seek my face, seek my kingdom, and I will lead you to righteousness.

"If my people who are called by my name humble themselves, and pray and seek my face and turn from their wicked ways, then I will hear from heaven and will forgive their sin and heal their land."

— *2 CHRONICLES 7:14, ESV*

I want to say it again; it only made you stronger. God wants to heal you. He wants to make you whole. He wants you to share your victories with someone else. Be a testimony to others so they can believe they can survive too. Anytime the enemy wants to plot and attack your emotions and your desires, he is trying to lead you astray, but God is still with you. God is faithful. He always does what He says He's going to do for your life. I know one thing, God saved my life. If I would have stayed on the same track, or stayed in the same territory, I would have lost everything I had…but God. He saved my life, and He'll save your life too. It's only going to make you stronger. Your cries are heard. He will make you anew. You're now walking in promotion, activation, and elevation. You're now walking with an ability that no one could ever take from you. You now have a new voice and a new attitude, a new vision, new perspective, and perseverance that'll lead you even further in your life. You are now mature and have gained wisdom.

You Are No Longer Blinded!

"In his kindness God called you to share in his eternal glory by means of Christ Jesus. So after you have suffered a little while, he will restore, support, and strengthen you, and he will place you on a firm foundation."

— *1 PETER 5:10*

Know this: You made it and now you can see clearly.

Daily Prayer: *"Father God, thank you for allowing me to become stronger because I've gained knowledge and strength through any storm."*

IT ONLY MADE YOU STRONGER!

ABOUT THE AUTHOR

Dr. JaVaski "JD" McDonald is a Texas native. Growing up in the church, service to others in God's name has always been a part of his mindset and personality. Dr. JD is a proud military veteran, and spent over 14 years in education, teaching and coaching at the high school and collegiate level. He earned his Bachelor's degree from Huston-Tillotson University, and a Master's degree from West Texas A&M University. He received a Doctorate degree at Concordia University and studied seminary at St. James Community Institute for Biblical Studies. Today, he is the founder and Senior Pastor of Aspire Generations Ministries. His ultimate goal is to aspire all generations to seek the Kingdom of God and accept the promise of God.

INFORMATION

Dr. JaVaski D. McDonald

Facebook.com/AspireGenerations

Instagram.com/AspireGenerations

Instagram.com/DrJaVaski

www.tiktok.com/@DrJaVaski

Bookings: DrJaVaski@gmail.com

AspireGenerations.org

ASPIRE
GENERATIONS
NETWORK

ASPIRE GENERATIONS NETWORK L.L.C

Made in the USA
Coppell, TX
01 March 2022

74250010R00044